THE
PRESIDENTS

KENNETH C. DAVIS
ILLUSTRATED BY PEDRO MARTIN

HarperCollins*Publishers*

ACKNOWLEDGMENTS

★ ★ ★ ★ ★

An author's name goes on the cover of a book. But behind that book are a great many people who make it all happen. I would like to thank all the wonderful people at HarperCollins who helped make this book a reality, including Susan Katz, Kate Morgan Jackson, Barbara Lalicki, Harriett Barton, Rosemary Brosnan, Anne Dunn, Dana Hayward, Maggie Herold, Esilda Kerr, Fumi Kosaka, Rachel Orr, and Katherine Rogers. I would also like to thank David Black, Joy Tutela, and Alix Reid for their friendship, assistance, and great ideas. My wife, Joann, and my children, Jenny and Colin, are always a source of inspiration, joy, and support. Without them, I could not do my work.

I would especially like to thank April Prince for her devoted efforts and unique contributions. This book would not have been possible without her tireless work, imagination, and creativity.

This is a Don't Know Much About® book. Don't Know Much About® is the trademark of Kenneth C. Davis.

Don't Know Much About® the Presidents

Copyright © 2002 by Kenneth C. Davis

Manufactured in China by South China Printing Company Ltd. All rights reserved.

www.harperchildrens.com

Library of Congress Cataloging-in-Publication Data
Davis, Kenneth C.
    Don't know much about the presidents / by Kenneth C. Davis ; illustrated by Pedro Martin.
      p.   cm.
    ISBN 0-06-028615-6 — ISBN 0-06-028616-4 (lib. bdg.) — ISBN 0-06-446231-5 (pbk.)
    1. Presidents—United States—History—Miscellanea—Juvenile literature. 2. Presidents—United States—Biography—Miscellanea—Juvenile literature. 3. United States—Politics and government—Miscellanea—Juvenile literature. [1. Presidents—Miscellanea. 2. United States—Politics and government—Miscellanea. 3. Questions and answers.] I. Martin, Pedro, date, ill. II. Title.
E176.1 .D38 2002
973'.09'9—dc21   00-046098
                                                                                          CIP
                                                                                          AC

Design by Charles Yuen

❖

"I pray Heaven to bestow the best Blessings on this House and all that shall hereafter inhabit it. May none but honest and wise men ever rule beneath this roof."

—John Adams, from his journal entry dated November 2, 1800, his second night in the White House

INTRODUCTION

Back when the United States of America was born, the patriots who rebelled against England got rid of a king named George. (He was George the Third, and you can read more about him in *Don't Know Much About® the Kings and Queens of England*.) America's first president was also named George (Washington, of course!). Then, in the year 2000, America started a new century by electing another president named George (Bush). His father was also president, and he was also named George Bush. But sorry—having the name George won't really help you become president.

How do you become president, and what does a president do? Is being president hard work? (The real answer is that some presidents work harder than others.) Are all the presidents good? Do the president's kids have to be careful not to mess up the White House?

Don't Know Much About® the Presidents tells the story of all forty-three of America's commanders in chief and their families. But this book is not just filled with dry dates and old names. Like every Don't Know Much About® book, it is loaded with questions and answers about extraordinary men and women, and the lives they led, that remind us that history is about real people doing real things. When you remember that, learning about our past becomes a lot more fun. By George!

Note: Dates in parentheses following a president's name refer to the years in which he served as president.

The Presidency of the United States

What is the president's job?

The president of the United States has one of the biggest and hardest jobs in the world. As the leader of one of the world's most powerful countries, the president

—runs the military as commander in chief of the armed forces

—negotiates *treaties,* or agreements, with other countries

—appoints Supreme Court justices and other judges

—proposes new laws and signs them into legislation when Congress passes them

—can veto bills that Congress passes

—appoints ambassadors to other countries and sets foreign policy

—helps decide how much money the government will spend each year

—appoints the heads of, and helps run, the government's many departments

A constitution is *a document that tells the laws of a country and the rights of the people who live there. The U.S. Constitution was written way back in 1787. Since then, there have been twenty-seven amendments, or changes, to the document. The first ten amendments, called the Bill of Rights, guarantee basic liberties such as "protection from unreasonable search and seizure" and freedom of religion and speech.*

★★★★★★★★★★★★★

After turning eighteen, any American citizen can register to vote.

Get me the Secretary of Recess!

PRESIDENT

Could *you* be president one day?

You could be! But you'll have to wait until you're thirty-five. The U.S. Constitution also says you must have been born a U.S. citizen and have lived in the United States at least fourteen years.

Is a presidential race run on a racetrack?

No, it's run all around the country, and on TV, the radio, and the Internet. In a presidential "race" anyone who wants to be president announces that he or she is a

candidate, or someone competing for election (also called "running for president.") Each candidate travels all over the country *campaigning,* or telling the American people what he or she will do if elected.

Can the president do anything he wants?

No way! The men who wrote the Constitution made sure that no one person or group would have too much power. They gave the government three *branches*, or departments, with equal power. The branches are

—**executive**: the president and his *cabinet,* or group of advisers
—**legislative**: the Senate and the House of Representatives, together called Congress
—**judicial**: courts and judges

Who chooses the president?

A president is elected every four years. The president isn't elected, or chosen, by a direct vote of the people. Instead, each state chooses a number of electors equal to its representation in Congress. (All the electors together are called the electoral college.) Those electors then vote for the president. Whichever candidate gets the most votes in the state gets all of that state's electoral votes. Once the votes are counted, a newly elected president has about two and a half months before he or she is *inaugurated,* or officially sworn in, at a ceremony at the U.S. Capitol on January 20.

What does the president get paid?

Today, he gets $400,000 a year plus expenses. That much money would get you into DisneyWorld every day for nearly thirty years! The president also gets:

—the use of a furnished house and a country retreat
—a limousine, yacht, and use of a private plane
—personal and office staff
—Secret Service agents to protect him from danger

GEORGE WASHINGTON [1789–1797]

"I WALK ON UNTRODDEN GROUND."

How did George Washington know how to be president?

He didn't, since he was the first one. But his countrymen believed in him. They wanted him to lead the new nation because he'd been the heroic general of the Continental Army, which won independence from Great Britain in the Revolutionary War.

After Washington was elected, no one knew what to call him. Some ideas were His Elective Majesty, His Elective Highness, Your Mightiness, and His Highness the President of the United States and Protector of the Rights of the Same. Phew! Good thing they just decided to call him Mr. President!

Why wasn't Washington made King George I of America?

He almost was. People liked George Washington so much that some wanted to crown him king. But Washington said he didn't want to be king of the United States. After all, Americans had just fought for their freedom because they didn't like being ruled by a king.

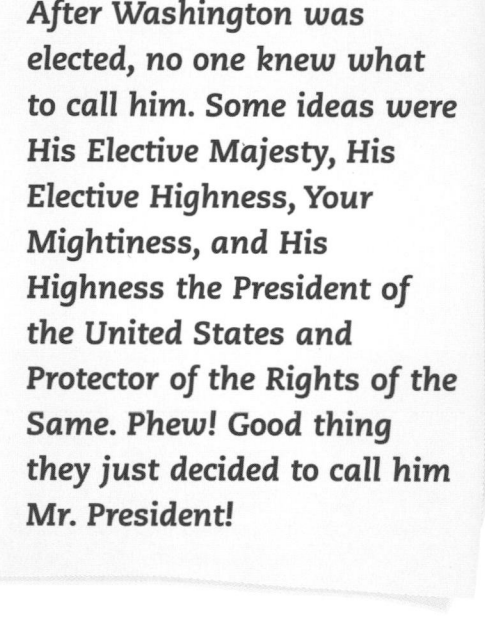

...We could also go with "Grand Pooh-bah," "High-muck-a-muck" or "Super-dude".

Why was Washington the only president who didn't live in Washington, D.C.?

The city wasn't built yet. Washington chose the site of the capital city that was named to honor him, but he himself lived in the temporary capitals of New York and Philadelphia.

Why didn't President Washington ever have a toothache?

By the time Washington became president, he had only one tooth of his own. A rumor said his false teeth were wooden, but actually they were made of elephant and walrus tusk and of cow, hippo, and even human teeth. What a mouthful!

Who wasn't too cheery about having his cherries chopped?

Legend says that when young George Washington's father asked what happened to one of his cherry trees, the future president said, "I can't tell a lie . . . I did cut it with my hatchet." In fact, a writer made up the story to show how honest Washington was.

What if we say the cherry tree attacked him first and that George had to defend himself...

Who did Washington call Sweetlips, Madame Moose, and True Love?

Not his wife, Martha, but his dogs! Washington was such an animal lover that he had his horses' teeth brushed every morning. Yet he himself, like most other people of his time, thought bathing was unhealthy and didn't do it very often!

Every President starting with George Washington has said the same oath at his inauguration: "I do solemnly swear that I will faithfully execute the office of president of the United States, and will, to the best of my ability, preserve, protect, and defend the Constitution of the United States." The president customarily adds "So help me God."

TIMELINE

1783	1787	1788	1789
American colonies win Revolutionary War against Great Britain	Delaware, Pennsylvania, and New Jersey become first three states	Georgia, Connecticut, Massachusetts, Maryland, South Carolina, New Hampshire, Virginia, and New York become fourth through eleventh states	North Carolina becomes twelfth state Washington declares first official Thanksgiving holiday War Department established by Congress

1790	1791	1792	1794	1796
Rhode Island becomes thirteenth state Washington, D.C., founded	Bill of Rights added to the Constitution Vermont becomes fourteenth state	First U.S. mint opens in Philadelphia, Pennsylvania Kentucky becomes fifteenth state	President Washington puts down Whiskey Rebellion	Tennessee becomes sixteenth state

JOHN ADAMS [1797–1801]

"A GOVERNMENT OF LAWS, AND NOT OF MEN."

Why did John Adams run for president?

During the Revolution, John Adams had helped pass the Declaration of Independence. He also helped make the treaty with England after the war. When George Washington was elected America's first president, John Adams was elected the first vice president. The vice president's main job is to fill in if anything happens to the president. But Adams wanted to be number one. So when Washington refused a third term, Adams ran for president himself.

Roly-poly Adams was short and fat. His nickname was "His Rotundity."

Abigail Adams believed in women's rights and asked her husband to "remember the ladies" when drafting America's Constitution.

Did President and Mrs. Adams get lost looking for the White House?

They did, because the house was surrounded by woods at the time. Adams and his wife, Abigail, were the first couple to live in what was then called the "President's House." When they moved in, the walls in the cold, unfinished mansion were still wet. Abigail hung her laundry in the mansion's bare East Room.

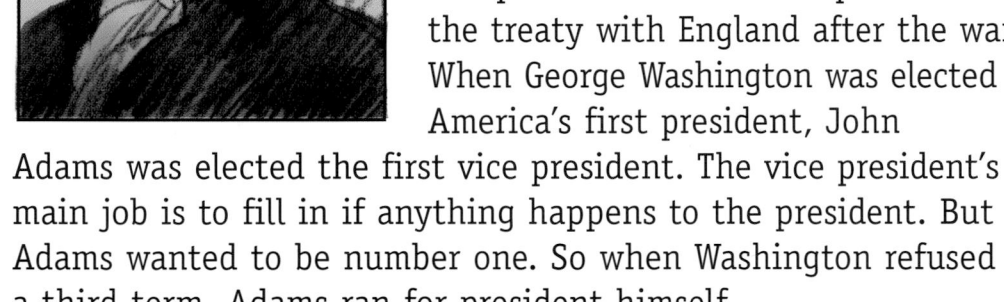

★★★★★★★★★★★★★★★★★★★★★★★★★★★

Adams passed away on the Fourth of July, 1826, exactly fifty years after the signing of the Declaration of Independence. It was his idea to celebrate the Fourth with "games, sports, guns, bells, bonfires, and illuminations" or fireworks.

 **TIMELINE**

1798	1799	1800	1800
U.S. Navy established	George Washington dies. He suffered acute laryngitis after a ride in the snow and rain, was bled heavily, and died. (At that time, doctors believed that illness was in the blood and getting rid of "bad blood" was a cure.)	Washington, D.C., made U.S. capital. John and Abigail Adams become the first occupants of the White House	Library of Congress, now the largest library in the world, established

THOMAS JEFFERSON [1801–1809]

> "... A LITTLE REBELLION, NOW AND THEN, IS A GOOD THING ..."

What did Jefferson have at the White House that barely any American had ever seen?

Grizzly bears. The bears came from land in the West that the U.S. bought from France in 1803 (called the Louisiana Purchase). The next year, Jefferson sent Meriwether Lewis and William Clark to explore the new territory. They returned with hundreds of plant and animal samples, including the bears, who lived in cages on the White House grounds.

★★★★★★★★★★★★★★★

The land from the Louisiana Purchase made the United States twice as big as it already was. It would later be divided into fifteen states.

Fill in the blank: Thomas Jefferson wrote, "All men are created _____."

Equal. This famous line is from the Declaration of Independence, which Jefferson wrote in 1776 to declare the American colonies free from Great Britain. Jefferson again upheld liberty by helping to pass the Virginia Statute of Religious Freedom, the first law in America that let people worship however they chose. But Jefferson felt his greatest achievement of all—even greater than being president—was founding the University of Virginia.

Will the real Thomas Jefferson please stand up?

Was Jefferson

a) an inventor who created the swivel chair, a type of pedometer, a walking stick that unfolded into a chair, a letter-copying device, and America's system of dollars and cents?

b) a scholar who spoke six languages?

c) a talented violinist and excellent singer who loved to dance?

d) a self-taught architect who built his own home, called Monticello, and designed the University of Virginia?

Believe it or not, Jefferson was all these things. Many people say he was America's most gifted president. He had unlimited curiosity and owned a huge library. "I cannot live without books," he said.

"To the shores of Tripoli" is a line from a famous song about the United States Marines. In 1804, Thomas Jefferson sent some American marines to attack Tripoli, a city in North Africa where pirates were holding American sailors for ransom. After that brief war, these Barbary pirates agreed to stop kidnapping sailors for ransom.

Are there streamers and noisemakers at a political party?

Actually, a political party isn't a celebration. A *political party* is a group of people who share certain ideas about how to run the country. Jefferson started the group that today we call the *Democratic* party. The other main party in the United States nowadays is the modern *Republican* party.

What food did Americans think was poisonous until Jefferson ate some?

a) cheeseburgers   c) potato chips
b) tomatoes   d) lima beans

The answer is *b*. Besides growing tomatoes for food, Jefferson also served the first french fries in America at his home, Monticello.

What did Jefferson have in common with President John Adams?

Both ex-presidents died on the same day—the Fourth of July, 1826—just hours apart.

TIMELINE

1803	1804	1806	1808
Louisiana Purchase Ohio becomes seventeenth state	Lewis and Clark leave to explore Louisiana Territory	Noah Webster publishes first American dictionary Gas streetlights introduced	Slave trade banned, meaning that no new slaves can be brought to America

JAMES MADISON [1809–1817]

> "THE HAPPY UNION OF THESE STATES IS A WONDER;
> THEIR CONSTITUTION IS A MIRACLE; THEIR EXAMPLE THE
> HOPE OF LIBERTY THROUGHOUT THE WORLD."

How was James Madison a father if he didn't have any children?

Before he became president, Madison earned the name "Father of the Constitution" because many ideas in the document were his. He also drafted the Bill of Rights.

Why did Madison's friends say he was "no bigger than a half piece of soap"?

Because he stood only five feet four inches and weighed less than one hundred pounds, making him America's smallest president.

How did the White House get its name?

Soon after it was built, newspaper reporters started calling the President's House the White House because it was painted white. Good thing the house isn't blue with red polka dots!

What's a "first lady"?

The president's wife. First ladies aren't elected or paid, but they often work very hard. They entertain guests at important events and often work for causes like teaching people to read or raising awareness about a disease. Madison's popular wife, Dolley, was the first president's wife to be called first lady. She is especially remembered for saving a famous portrait of George Washington when the British burned the White House in 1814.

TIMELINE

1812	1814	1815	1816
War of 1812 against Britain begins	Francis Scott Key writes the words to "The Star-Spangled Banner"	War of 1812 ends	Indiana becomes nineteenth state
Louisiana becomes eighteenth state			

JAMES MONROE [1817–1825]

> "NATIONAL HONOR IS NATIONAL PROPERTY OF THE HIGHEST VALUE."

Where did James Monroe go that no president had gone before?

On a tour of the country just after his inauguration, President Monroe traveled as far north as Portland, Maine, and as far west as Detroit, Michigan. Cheering crowds greeted him everywhere, in what was called an "Era of Good Feelings" in America.

Warning: Stay off our turf!

That's basically what the Monroe Doctrine said. President Monroe didn't want European countries butting into American affairs, so in 1823 he wrote a doctrine, or statement of government policy, that warned them not to start any new colonies in the Americas.

What territory did the U.S. buy from Spain during Monroe's term?

Hint: It's home to DisneyWorld and is now called the Sunshine State. That's right—Florida!

Monroe was the third president to die on the Fourth of July. He died in 1831, five years after John Adams and Thomas Jefferson.

TIMELINE

1817	1818	1819	1820	1821
Mississippi becomes twentieth state	Design of U.S. flag established	Alabama becomes twenty-second state	Maine becomes twenty-third state	Missouri becomes twenty-fourth state
	Illinois becomes twenty-first state		Missouri Compromise prohibits slavery in northern part of Louisiana Territory	

JOHN QUINCY ADAMS [1825–1829]

Wait, wasn't John Adams already president?

He was. But this was John Adams's son, John *Quincy* Adams. John Quincy was the first president to be the son of another president. Young John had an exciting childhood. When he was eight, he watched the Battle of Bunker Hill, the first real fighting of the Revolutionary War. Then he worked with his father in Europe. John Quincy always knew he wanted to be president one day.

What did President Adams wear when he swam in the Potomac River?

Nothing! (Bathing suits hadn't been invented yet.) Every morning at five o'clock, Adams hung his clothes on a tree and went for a swim. Once, his clothes were stolen. He had to ask a boy who was passing by to run to the White House and get him something else to wear!

Adams brought two new things to the White House: a pet alligator and a pool table.

Which house did Adams go to when he left the White House?

John Quincy Adams became the only president to return to the House of Representatives, where he devoted himself to fighting slavery.

★ ★ ★ ★ ★ ★ ★ ★ ★ ★ ★ ★ ★

Like his father, John Quincy Adams loved poetry. The sixth president once said, "Could I have chosen my own genius and condition, I should have made myself a great poet."

TIMELINE

1825	1828
Erie Canal opens, letting boats travel from the Great Lakes to the Atlantic Ocean	Work begins on the nation's first steam-powered railroad, the Baltimore & Ohio

ANDREW JACKSON [1829–1837]

> ## "ONE MAN WITH COURAGE MAKES A MAJORITY."

Who believed that if Andrew Jackson could become president, anyone could?

Lots of Americans felt that way, because Jackson was different from the presidents before him. He was born in a log cabin on the *frontier*, or new American West. His parents were poor, and both died by the time he was fourteen. Jackson joined the army and worked his way up. People liked that Jackson was a common man who had succeeded by working hard.

Why did President Jackson leave his own inauguration party?

Because it got so wild and crazy. More than twenty thousand fans poured into the White House through the doors—and windows! Poor Jackson was almost suffocated. He finally had to slip out and spend the night in a hotel.

★★★★★★★★★★★★★★

Jackson's soldiers gave him the nickname "Old Hickory" because they said he was as tough as the wood of a hickory tree.

Jackson was a friend to Native Americans.

False. As a military officer, Jackson fought many battles *against* Native Americans. Soon after he became president, he signed the Indian Removal Act and started forcing the Cherokee and other tribes to leave their homelands in the South for reservations in the West.

Jackson was the first president to ride on a train.

What did Jackson have removed from his arm while he was president?

a) a tattoo

b) a sliver of wood

c) a bullet

d) a whole bunch of freckles

It's letter *c*. Old Hickory had two bullets in his body from the approximately one hundred duels he fought before he became president. One stayed lodged near his heart for the rest of his life.

Did Jackson fight any duels as president?

No, but someone did try to *assassinate*, or kill, him while he was in office. The man shot at Jackson with two different guns, but amazingly, both misfired. The feisty president chased after the man, shaking his cane.

TIMELINE

1829	1831	1833	1835	1836
Typewriter invented	Nat Turner's slave rebellion in Virginia	The Anti-Slavery Society created, formally beginning the battle to end slavery in the U.S.	Seminole Indians in Florida rebel against the U.S. government Halley's Comet passes by Earth	Arkansas becomes twenty-fifth state Davy Crockett and 182 others die fighting for Texas's independence from Mexico at the Alamo in Texas

MARTIN VAN BUREN [1837–1841]

TRUE OR FALSE Martin Van Buren was the first president to be born an American citizen.

True. All the presidents before Van Buren were originally British citizens, having been born before the United States became its own country. So it's funny that Van Buren spoke Dutch at home as a child. (His family had moved to the U.S. from Holland.)

What made President Van Buren an "O.K." candidate?

The saying "O.K." may have come from Van Buren's 1840 reelection campaign. Van Buren grew up in Kinderhook—sometimes called Old Kinderhook—New York. Old Kinderhook, or "O.K.," clubs supported him as a candidate who was "O.K.!"

I'm O.K.! You're O.K.!

What did many Americans lose during Van Buren's presidency?

Their jobs. In 1837, the United States was in a big *economic depression*, or time when business is bad and many people are out of work. The depression wasn't Van Buren's fault, but he took a lot of the blame anyway. The president loved expensive things, and some people criticized him for living in luxury while Americans starved.

TIMELINE

1837	1838–1839
Michigan becomes twenty-sixth state Samuel Morse patents the telegraph	The Five Civilized Tribes—Cherokee, Chickasaw, Choctaw, Creek, and Seminole—are forced west on the Trail of Tears

WILLIAM HENRY HARRISON [1841]

> ". . . THE ONLY LEGITIMATE RIGHT TO GOVERN IS AN EXPRESS GRANT OF POWER FROM THE GOVERNED."

Did William Henry Harrison always want to be president?

No. Harrison studied to become a doctor until he ran out of money for school. So he went into politics instead, having grown up around politicians. His father was a signer of the Declaration of Independence and a friend of George Washington, who often visited the Harrison plantation.

Get some rest and vote for me in the morning.

The long and short of Harrison's presidency . . .

Harrison gave the longest inauguration speech in presidential history—it lasted nearly two hours! Inauguration day was cold and rainy, and Harrison didn't wear a coat. He died of pneumonia thirty-one days later. His term was the shortest of any president's.

Harrison had been a general in the army. He was nicknamed "Old Tippecanoe" after he defeated the Shawnee Indians under Chief Tecumseh at the Tippecanoe River in 1811.

President Harrison's ten children gave him forty-eight grand- and great-grandchildren—far more than any other president. (Watch for one of those grandsons later in this book. . . .)

☀ TIMELINE

1841

Supreme Court rules that captured Africans who rebelled on board the *Amistad* are free, not slaves

JOHN TYLER [1841–1845]

If he wasn't elected president, how did John Tyler get the job?

When William Henry Harrison died in office, Tyler became the first vice president to assume the presidency. Many people thought "His Accidency," as they called Tyler, would just pretend to be president until the next election. But instead, Tyler became a real president, setting the example for all vice presidents after him. To prove that he was really president, Tyler returned unopened all mail that was addressed to him as "Acting President."

What was Tyler doing when he found out he was president?

a) leading soldiers in battle

b) writing an important speech

c) playing marbles with his sons

d) visiting kings and queens in Europe

Stories say the answer is letter *c*. President Tyler loved children. Maybe that's why he had more than any other president—fifteen! Tyler gave several parties at the White House for his children, his grandchildren, and their friends.

President Tyler's granddaughter Letitia was the first girl born in the White House, in 1842.

TIMELINE

1845
Florida becomes twenty-seventh state

JAMES K. POLK [1845–1849]

> "NO PRESIDENT WHO PERFORMS HIS DUTIES FAITHFULLY AND CONSCIENTIOUSLY CAN HAVE ANY LEISURE."

On a scale of one to ten, how much fun was James K. Polk's inauguration party?

If you must have fun, I recommend a short nap followed by a rousing game of sitting quietly.

Probably a ten—until the president and his wife arrived. Because of her religious beliefs, First Lady Sarah Polk didn't allow drinking, dancing, or card playing at the White House during her husband's presidency.

Oh, honey, guess what I bought today!

TRUE OR FALSE **Polk was the first American president to govern from coast to coast.**

True. Polk settled an argument about the U.S.–Canadian border with Great Britain, which gave America land that is now Oregon and Washington. As a result, America finally stretched from the Atlantic Ocean to the Pacific Ocean. Polk also bought land from Mexico that would become California, New Mexico, Arizona, Utah, Nevada, and parts of Colorado and Wyoming.

Polk may have worked harder than any other president. He died just three months after leaving office, apparently worn out.

TIMELINE

1845	1846	1846	1846–1848	1847	1848	1840s–1850s
Texas becomes twenty-eighth state	Iowa becomes twenty-ninth state	The first professional baseball game is played in Hoboken, New Jersey	Mexican War fought over Texas's southern border	First U.S. postage stamps issued	Wisconsin becomes thirtieth state	Thousands of Americans move west via covered wagon on the Oregon and Santa Fe Trails

ZACHARY TAYLOR [1849–1850]

How many votes did Zachary Taylor cast for himself?

None! Taylor never voted in a presidential election. Before his presidency, he was a professional soldier who was always on the move and thus didn't have a hometown in which to vote. Taylor wasn't a big fan of politics, but so many people wanted him to run for president that he agreed to serve his country.

What made Taylor "Old Rough and Ready"?

His soldiers called him that because of the twenty-five years he spent living on the frontier and fighting Native Americans. When Taylor became president, he wore the same dirty clothes he'd worn on his farm!

Well, I guess it's better than being called "Old Stinky and Wrinkly."

Are cherries and milk a good summertime treat?

For some people, but not for President Taylor. After spending a hot summer day at the Washington Monument, the president ate a big bowl of cherries and drank a pitcher of iced milk. He died five days later of sunstroke or food poisoning, no one knows which.

President Taylor brought his favorite horse, Whitey, to the White House. Whitey grazed on the lawn until souvenir hunters pulled hairs from his tail and he had to be put in a stable.

TIMELINE

1849

California gold rush begins

Walter Hunt patents safety pin

Harriet Tubman escapes from slavery and goes on to lead more than three hundred slaves to freedom on the Underground Railroad

MILLARD FILLMORE [1850–1853]

> "IT IS A NATIONAL DISGRACE THAT OUR PRESIDENTS . . . SHOULD BE CAST ADRIFT, AND PERHAPS BE COMPELLED TO KEEP A CORNER GROCERY STORE FOR SUBSISTENCE."

Fillmore sent Matthew Perry, a naval commodore, to Japan in 1853. Perry's visit led the Japanese to trade with the United States, and eventually with European countries, for the first time in over two hundred years.

What was installed in the White House during Millard Fillmore's presidency?

a) a disco ball

b) a stove

c) running water

d) a bowling alley

The answers are *b* and *c*.

Before Fillmore was president, the White House had only an open fire for cooking meals. When the stove arrived, no one—not even the cook—knew how to use it! Fillmore did figure out how to enjoy a bath with running water.

Where did the Underground Railroad go?

The Underground Railroad wasn't a real railroad, but a network of courageous people who helped slaves secretly travel from the South to the North. In 1850, President Fillmore signed the Fugitive Slave Act, which made it illegal to help a slave run away and required officials to return escaped slaves to their owners.

☀ TIMELINE

1850	1851	1852
Compromise of 1850 admits California, the thirty-first state, as a free state	Isaac Singer patents continuous-stitch sewing machine	Brown paper bag invented Harriet Beecher Stowe publishes her antislavery novel *Uncle Tom's Cabin* Elevator invented

FRANKLIN PIERCE [1853–1857]

Why did reporters call Franklin Pierce's wife "the shadow in the White House"?

Because First Lady Jane Pierce didn't go out in public for the first two years of her husband's term—not even to attend his inauguration. She was too sad. All three of the Pierces' sons had died. Their eleven-year-old boy died in a train accident right in front of his parents' eyes just a few days before President Pierce took office.

Pierce was so good at giving speeches that he memorized all 3,319 words of his inaugural address. That would be like memorizing the first seventeen pages of this book!

Why did President Pierce worry about the United States?

Because Americans had been arguing about slavery for years, and Pierce feared the issue might tear the country apart. People in Kansas were already fighting over whether the territory would become a free state or a slave state. More than two hundred people died in the controversy that became known as "Bleeding Kansas."

TIMELINE

1853	1854
Potato chips invented	Kansas-Nebraska Act overrules the Missouri Compromise, stating that each new state would decide for itself whether to allow slavery

15

JAMES BUCHANAN [1857–1861]

> "IF YOU ARE AS HAPPY, MY DEAR SIR, ON ENTERING THIS HOUSE AS I AM IN LEAVING IT, YOU ARE THE HAPPIEST MAN IN THE COUNTRY."

President Buchanan was the only president who never had a

a) temper tantrum

b) wife

c) pair of Rollerblades

d) cold

The answer is letter *b*. Since Buchanan had no first lady, he asked his niece, Miss Harriet Lane, to serve as White House hostess.

C'mon, Alabama. We're leaving!

S. Carolina

Alabama

Ohio

TRUE OR FALSE The United States shrank while Buchanan was president.

True. Even though Minnesota and Oregon were admitted to the *Union*, or United States, during Buchanan's presidency, seven states actually *left* the Union during his term. Slavery became such a big issue that South Carolina led six other Southern states to *secede* from, or leave, the Union in early 1861. By the end of the year, a total of eleven states would have seceded. War was in the air.

TIMELINE

1857	1858	1859	1860	1861
Supreme Court's *Dred Scott* decision declares slavery legal in all Western territories not yet states	President Buchanan sends message to England's Queen Victoria over first transatlantic cable Minnesota becomes thirty-second state	Oregon becomes thirty-third state John Brown leads antislavery raid on Harpers Ferry, Virginia	Pony Express begins cross-country mail delivery South Carolina secedes from the Union	Kansas becomes thirty-fourth state

27

Abraham Lincoln [1861–1865]

> "I BELIEVE THIS GOVERNMENT CANNOT ENDURE PERMANENTLY HALF SLAVE AND HALF FREE."

What did Abraham Lincoln help build when he was only seven years old?

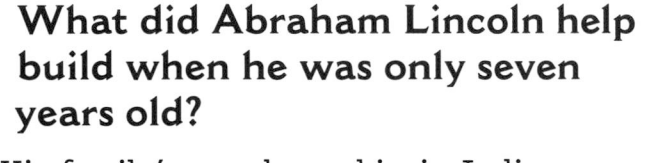

His family's new log cabin in Indiana. The family had just moved from their one-room, dirt-floor log cabin in Kentucky, where Lincoln was born. Young Lincoln had only one year of formal schooling, but he read every book he could get his hands on. He had jobs as a ferryboat captain, postmaster, country store clerk, and self-taught lawyer, but said, "From my boyhood up, it was my ambition to be president."

Why was another president elected while Lincoln was president?

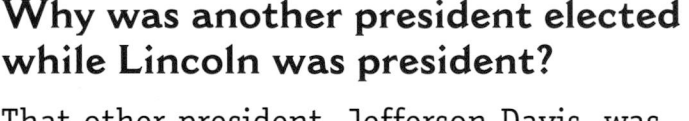

That other president, Jefferson Davis, was elected to lead the eleven Southern states that had left the Union. Those states had formed the Confederate States of America, or the *Confederacy*. It wasn't long before the Union and the Confederacy were fighting each other in an awful civil war. The South fought for their right to own slaves. The Union fought because Lincoln and others didn't think the Southern states had a right to secede. Lincoln especially was determined to keep the United States together as one country.

 **Lincoln liked the nickname "Abe."**

False. Even though "Honest Abe," as President Lincoln is often called, *was* trustworthy and hardworking, Lincoln hated being called Abe. No one called him that in his presence. Friends and family called him Mr. Lincoln, or just Lincoln.

Lincoln was America's tallest president. He was six feet four inches but looked even taller when he wore his stovepipe hat—in which he kept some of his important papers!

Where in Gettysburg, Pennsylvania, did Lincoln give his Gettysburg Address?

a) on a battlefield

b) at the barber shop

c) in a swimming pool

d) at a cemetery

Both *a* and *d*. Lincoln gave his famous speech at the dedication of a cemetery on the Civil War battlefield at Gettysburg. His famous 272-word address begins, "Four score and seven years ago our fathers brought forth on this continent a new nation, conceived in liberty, and dedicated to the proposition that all men are created equal." (*Score* means twenty, so four score and seven equals eighty-seven.).

Did Lincoln free the slaves?

No. He did issue the Emancipation Proclamation in 1863, which freed slaves in the Confederacy. The proclamation was sent out to newspapers and read aloud to crowds of people. But Lincoln couldn't really enforce laws in the Confederate States, since the Confederacy had its own president. The Thirteenth Amendment would officially free the slaves shortly after Lincoln's death in 1865.

What happened five days after the Union won the Civil War?

President Lincoln was assassinated by an actor named John Wilkes Booth. Booth, who wanted the Confederacy to win the war, shot the president during a play at Ford's Theater in Washington, D.C. Lincoln was the first president to be assassinated.

TIMELINE

1861	1863	1864	1865
Mississippi, Florida, Alabama, Georgia, Louisiana, Texas, Virginia, Arkansas, Tennessee, and North Carolina secede from Union and with South Carolina form the Confederate States of America	President Lincoln issues Emancipation Proclamation and gives Gettysburg Address	Nevada becomes thirty-sixth state	Civil War ends
Civil War begins when Confederates fire on Union-held Fort Sumter, near Charleston, South Carolina	West Virginia becomes thirty-fifth state		

ANDREW JOHNSON [1865–1869]

> "IF THE RABBLE WERE LOPPED OFF AT ONE END AND THE ARISTOCRAT AT THE OTHER, ALL WOULD BE WELL WITH THE COUNTRY."

Was Andrew Johnson a presidential handyman?

In a way. The Civil War was over, but the United States was a broken country. Land and cities, especially in the South, had been torn apart.

Families and communities were divided because brothers, friends, and neighbors had fought against one another in the war. Johnson had been vice president only forty-one days when President Lincoln was shot, and he was left to tackle the difficult job of *Reconstruction*, or repairing and uniting the nation, on his own.

What happens if a president eats too much fruit?

He gets impeached! Actually, that's not true. *Impeached* means accused of a crime. Johnson was the first president to be impeached. He was accused of breaking the law, because many congressmen thought he was being too nice to the South after the war. He was found not guilty by just one vote. No hard feelings about the close vote, though—years later he became the only ex-president elected to the Senate.

TRUE OR FALSE Andrew Johnson knew how to knit.

False. But he did know how to sew. Johnson started working in a tailor's shop when he was twelve. Since he never went to school, his wife taught him to read, write, and do math.

At his request Johnson was buried wrapped in an American flag and with a copy of the Constitution beneath his head.

TIMELINE

1865	1867	1868
Thirteenth Amendment abolishes slavery	Nebraska becomes thirty-seventh state U.S. buys Alaska from Russia for two cents an acre	Louisa May Alcott's *Little Women* published

ULYSSES S. GRANT [1869–1877]

> "NO TERMS EXCEPT AN UNCONDITIONAL AND IMMEDIATE SURRENDER CAN BE ACCEPTED."

Do generals generally make good presidents?

Sometimes, but not in Grant's case. Grant served as a general in the Union army, and his many victories ended the Civil War. But as president, Grant left decisions to other men and didn't realize they were lying and cheating right under his nose.

TRUE OR FALSE **If the president breaks the law, he isn't punished.**

False. If a president breaks the law, he can be arrested or fined just like anyone else. Grant was the only president to get a speeding ticket—while driving a horse! His horse and buggy were taken away and he had to walk the rest of the way home. He later paid a twenty-dollar fine.

Grant spent much of his life on horseback. When he was five years old, he could ride standing up on a horse's back like a circus performer!

TIMELINE

1869	1870–1900	1870	1871	1872
Transcontinental railroad completed	More than eleven million immigrants come to the United States	Fifteenth amendment gives former slaves and people of color the right to vote	P. T. Barnum's circus, "The Greatest Show on Earth," opens	President Grant helps create Yellowstone National Park, America's first national park
				Victoria Woodhull, the first female presidential candidate, and Frederick Douglass, the first black vice-presidential candidate, run for office

1873	1874	1876
Levi Straus sells first blue jeans	Elephant becomes symbol of Republican party	Colorado becomes thirty-eighth state
		United States celebrates its one hundredth birthday
		Alexander Graham Bell invents telephone
		Mark Twain writes *The Adventures of Tom Sawyer*
		General Custer defeated by Sioux and Cheyenne warriors at Little Bighorn

RUTHERFORD B. HAYES [1877–1881]

How could Rutherford B. Hayes have been born in both Delaware and Ohio?

He was born in the city of Delaware, Ohio!

How many people did President Hayes call on his new telephone?

Uh, sorry, you have the wrong number. Maybe you should try "2."

Not many—phones were so new that barely anyone had them! Hayes was the first president to use one in the White House. His phone number was "1."

Was "Lemonade Lucy" a sour first lady?

Hayes's wife, Lucy, earned that nickname because she was a religious woman who served lemonade instead of alcoholic beverages at White House events. But that didn't mean she didn't like to have fun. She started the White House Easter Egg Roll in 1878, and since then children have rolled their decorated eggs down the president's lawn each spring.

★★★★★★★★★★★★★★★

Newspapers called President Hayes "His Fraudulency" because many Americans believed his election had been rigged. Indeed, the vote was so close that the election had to be decided in Congress. In order to become president, Hayes had to promise so many things that he lost most of his power before he even took office.

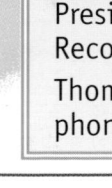

TIMELINE

1877	1879
President Hayes ends period of Reconstruction in the South	Thomas Edison invents electric lightbulb
Thomas Edison invents phonograph	

JAMES A. GARFIELD [1881]

"THE ELEVATION OF THE NEGRO RACE FROM SLAVERY TO THE FULL RIGHTS OF CITIZENSHIP IS THE MOST IMPORTANT POLITICAL CHANGE WE HAVE KNOWN SINCE THE ADOPTION OF THE CONSTITUTION."

What did James Garfield do for the last ten weeks of his presidency?

He lay in bed. Garfield had been president for less than four months when he was shot by one of his own supporters. The man thought his loyalty should have been rewarded with a government job. But Garfield believed those jobs should go to deserving people, not to friends and supporters. Garfield lived for eleven weeks after the shooting, but doctors couldn't save him.

How old was President Garfield when he learned to read?

He was just three years old! So it probably won't surprise you to learn that Garfield was a teacher and then a college president before becoming president of the United States.

Could President Garfield write with both hands?

Yes—at the same time! He could even write in a different language with each hand. To amuse guests, he wrote in Greek with one hand and Latin with the other. Try *that* at your next party!

TIMELINE

1881

First color photographs

Outlaw Billy the Kid shot down in New Mexico Territory

Clara Barton founds American Red Cross

CHESTER A. ARTHUR [1881–1885]

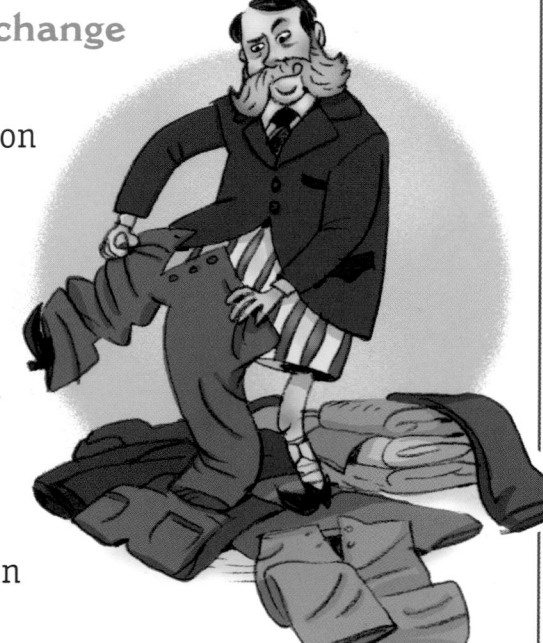

What did President Arthur change several times a day?

a) his pants

c) the radio station

b) his mind

d) his e-mail password

The answer is letter *a*. Chester Arthur had eighty pairs of pants! "Elegant Arthur," as he was called, also redecorated the White House before he moved in so that it would be up to his spiffy standards. Arthur sold twenty-four wagonloads of priceless presidential furniture and belongings, including one of John Quincy Adams's hats and a pair of Lincoln's pants.

Was President Arthur ever a teacher?

Yes, as a young man. And he continued to give exams even as president! Arthur agreed with President Garfield's belief that government jobs should be given to the most qualified people. He created difficult tests applicants had to pass to earn their jobs.

What sport had President Arthur hooked?

Fishing. President Arthur was one of the best fishermen in America. An eighty-pound bass he caught off the coast of Rhode Island was one of the biggest fish ever caught in that region. The fish was probably as big as you are!

TIMELINE

1880s	1883	1884	1885
First laws passed to regulate child labor and improve working conditions	"Buffalo Bill's Wild West Show" begins Brooklyn Bridge completed	Mark Twain writes *The Adventures of Huckleberry Finn*	Washington Monument dedicated in Washington, D.C.

GROVER CLEVELAND [1885–1889, 1893–1897]

"Just a minute, I'll see if I'm in."

Cleveland

Who answered the White House phones for Grover Cleveland?

President Cleveland did it himself at the beginning of his first term! Cleveland wanted to do *everything* himself. No wonder he was often at his desk until two or three o'clock in the morning.

Cleveland was the only president to serve two terms that weren't in a row.

★★★★★★★★★★★★★

At the end of President Cleveland's first term, his wife, Frances, told White House domestic staff, "I want everything just the way it is now when we come back. That will be exactly four years from now." Though the staff was probably surprised, the first lady was right!

TRUE OR FALSE **The Baby Ruth candy bar was named after the great baseball player Babe Ruth.**

False. It was named after Ruth Cleveland, the president's popular older daughter. Cleveland's younger daughter, Esther, was also well known. Esther was the first child born to a president and first lady in the White House.

Why did President Cleveland have sneaky surgery?

Shhh! President Cleveland had secret, life-saving surgery on a boat in the middle of the night during his second term. The president had cancer of the mouth, but he didn't want Americans to know and worry about him. Doctors removed part of Cleveland's jaw and replaced it with rubber. No one learned about the operation until after Cleveland died.

 **True or false: President Cleveland is pictured on the one-dollar bill.**

False; that's George Washington. Cleveland is shown on another bank note—the thousand-dollar bill!

Cleveland was the only president to be married in the White House. He had known his bride, Frances Fulsom, since she was born. (Frances was the daughter of Cleveland's former business partner.) In fact, he bought her her first baby carriage!

TIMELINE

1885	1886	1888
First term: World's first skyscraper, the Home Insurance Company Building, ten stories tall, built in Chicago	Statue of Liberty dedicated Geronimo surrenders, ending fighting between U.S. and Apache Indians Coca-Cola first produced in Atlanta, Georgia	George Eastman invents the Kodak camera

1893	1894	1895	1896
Second term: Cracker Jack introduced	Thomas Edison introduces first motion pictures President Cleveland sends troops to break up strike by Pullman railroad car workers in Chicago	John Harvey Kellogg invents cornflakes in Battle Creek, Michigan	Utah becomes forty-fifth state Klondike gold rush in Alaska First Sunday newspaper comics

BENJAMIN HARRISON [1889–1893]

Benjamin Harrison grew up on the farm of which U.S. president?

Hint: It's the president who had more grand- and great-grandchildren than any other. He also happened to be Benjamin Harrison's grandfather. It was William Henry Harrison, America's ninth president. When "Little Ben," who was only five and a half feet tall, campaigned for president, he said, "Grandfather's hat fits!"

Was President Harrison afraid of the dark?

No, he was afraid of the lights! Electric light was installed in the White House during his term. Before that there had been only candles and gas light. It's said that both the president and the first lady were so afraid of getting an electric shock from the lights that they didn't turn them on for weeks!

How was President Harrison like an iceberg?

Harrison was sometimes called the "human iceberg" because he was so stiff and formal when he met strangers. But once he got to know a person, he was warm and kind.

First Lady Caroline Harrison was the first to put up a Christmas tree in the White House.

☀ TIMELINE

1889	1890	1891	1892
North Dakota, South Dakota, Montana, and Washington become thirty-ninth through forty-second states	Sioux Indians massacred by U.S. troops at Wounded Knee Idaho and Wyoming become forty-third and forty-fourth states	First basketball game played, in Springfield, Massachusetts	First automobile built

WILLIAM McKINLEY [1897–1901]

"WAR SHOULD NEVER BE ENTERED UPON UNTIL EVERY AGENCY OF PEACE HAS FAILED."

Did President McKinley prefer buttons, snaps, or zippers?

William McKinley liked buttons— campaign buttons. He was the first presidential candidate to use them. McKinley was kind, smart, and well liked. He always knew what he wanted. He said, "I have never been in doubt since I was old enough to think intelligently that I would someday be made president."

TRUE OR FALSE **McKinley had a pet parrot who could whistle "Yankee Doodle."**

True! If the president whistled the first part of the tune, the parrot would finish it.

What was President McKinley's good-luck charm?

A red carnation he wore on his suit coat. It didn't bring him any luck on September 6, 1901, however. That day, the president had just bent down to give his carnation to a little girl when an *anarchist*, someone who doesn't believe in government, shot him. McKinley died eight days later, the third president to be assassinated.

⚙ TIMELINE

1897	1898	1900
America's first subway opens, in Boston	Puerto Rico, the Philippines, and Guam become American islands after the Spanish-American War	Hawaii annexed by United States

Olds Company in Detroit, Michigan, begins mass production of cars |

THEODORE ROOSEVELT [1901–1909]

"SPEAK SOFTLY AND CARRY A BIG STICK."

What did President Theodore Roosevelt do after a busy day at the White House?

He jogged around the Washington Monument. Having been a weak and sickly child, Roosevelt was a very active adult. He played tennis, practiced judo, took boxing lessons, hiked, hunted, swam, and climbed mountains.

TRUE OR FALSE Roosevelt was a self-taught cowboy.

True! After his mother and first wife died on the same day in 1884, Roosevelt overcame his grief by spending two years as a cattle rancher in the Dakota Territory.

What did President Roosevelt do with 7,800 miles?

He got rid of them. Roosevelt arranged to acquire land in Central America so America could build the Panama Canal, a man-made waterway that connects the Atlantic and Pacific Oceans. The shortcut means ships don't have to sail the nearly 8,000 miles around South America.

Were Roosevelt's Rough Riders a motorcycle gang?

No, they were a group of volunteers Roosevelt rounded up to help Cuba fight for independence during the Spanish-American War. Reports said Roosevelt led the men on a heroic horseback charge up Cuba's San Juan Hill. But the "charge" must have been on foot, because transportation problems had forced the men to leave their horses back in Florida!

Roosevelt, who was just forty-two years old when President McKinley died, is still the youngest man to have held the office of U.S. president.

In an important step for race relations, Roosevelt brought African-American educator Booker T. Washington to the White House for dinner.

Could Americans trust Roosevelt?

Roosevelt was a "trustbuster," but that didn't mean he was dishonest. A *trust* is a large company that owns many smaller companies; it is a kind of monopoly. For instance, the Standard Oil trust owned 90 percent of America's oil businesses. When one company gets so big, it can be bad for *consumers*, the people who need to buy its products. The Antitrust Act tried to make big businesses fair to other businesses and responsible to the public. As president, Roosevelt tried hard to enforce the antitrust laws, and he became known as the "trustbuster."

Was Teddy Roosevelt named after the Teddy Bear?

No, the bear was named after him! The stuffed bear got its name after Roosevelt refused to shoot a bear cub while on a hunting trip. The nature-loving Roosevelt was a *conservationist* who preserved more national forests and created more national parks than any other president.

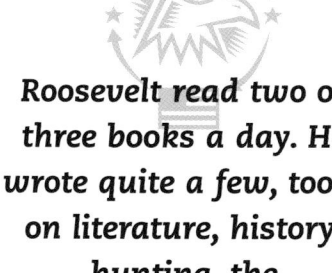

Roosevelt read two or three books a day. He wrote quite a few, too— on literature, history, hunting, the wilderness, America, and ranch life.

Which activities did Roosevelt's children do in the White House?

a) roller skate and walk on stilts in the hallways

b) slide down the main staircase on cookie sheets

c) keep a one-legged rooster, a snake, a parrot, a pony, a bear, and a guinea pig as pets

d) take their pony up the elevator

e) all of the above

Roosevelt's six kids had as much energy as their father—the answer is letter *e*!

Roosevelt was the first president to ride in a car, fly in a plane, and go underwater in a submarine.

TIMELINE

1901	1903	1904	1906	1907
U.S. citizenship granted to Native Americans of the Five Civilized Tribes	Wright Brothers fly first airplane at Kitty Hawk, North Carolina	Construction begins on Panama Canal Ice cream cones become popular	Meat Inspection and Pure Food and Drug Acts passed to protect Americans' health San Francisco earthquake	First Mother's Day celebrated Oklahoma becomes forty-sixth state

WILLIAM HOWARD TAFT [1909–1913]

> "[AFRICAN AMERICANS'] ANCESTORS CAME HERE YEARS AGO AGAINST THEIR WILL, AND THIS IS THEIR ONLY COUNTRY AND THEIR ONLY FLAG. THEY HAVE SHOWN THEMSELVES ANXIOUS TO LIVE FOR IT AND TO DIE FOR IT."

Where in the White House did President Taft get stuck?

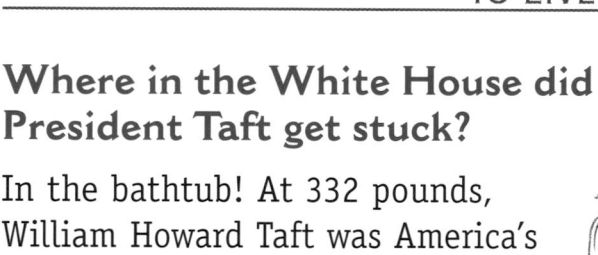

In the bathtub! At 332 pounds, William Howard Taft was America's heaviest president. A new bathtub—one big enough to fit four regular-sized men—had to be installed just for him.

Did Taft have a ball being president?

He did. *Base*ball, that is. Despite his size, Taft enjoyed tennis and dancing and was one of America's best presidential baseball players. Taft created the tradition of throwing the first ball at baseball games. He also accidentally started the "seventh-inning stretch" when he stood up to stretch in the seventh inning. Other people stood, too, out of respect and realized it felt good to get up.

★★★★★★★★★★★★★★★★★

Taft and Teddy Roosevelt were good friends, and many people thought President Taft would continue Roosevelt's policies instead of starting his own. They said Taft's name meant Take Advice From Teddy.

What did President Taft really want to be when he grew up?

Taft wanted to be a justice on the Supreme Court, the highest court in the nation. Eight years after he served his term as president, busting trusts and protecting natural resources as Teddy Roosevelt had done, he finally got his dream job.

☀ TIMELINE

1910	1912
Boy Scouts of America established	New Mexico and Arizona become forty-seventh and forty-eighth states
First sneakers become popular	
Halley's Comet passes by Earth	*Titanic* sinks off the coast of Newfoundland

WOODROW WILSON [1913–1921]

"THE WORLD MUST BE MADE SAFE FOR DEMOCRACY."

What was Woodrow Wilson's wish for World War I?

That the United States could stay out of the war. Most of the world's powerful nations were fighting Germany and its *allies*, or friends, to keep them from taking over land that wasn't theirs. When German submarines sank American ships in 1917, however, Wilson had no choice but to fight back. After the war, Wilson tried unsuccessfully to create a League of Nations that would solve international problems by talking instead of fighting. After Wilson suffered a stroke, the United States Senate refused to join the League in November 1919 for political reasons, and the League was doomed to failure. Another league was finally started twenty-five years later as the United Nations.

Wilson once dreamed of being a stage performer. He sometimes imitated the singers and tap dancers he saw in musicals!

Who was "Mrs. President"?

That's what some people called First Lady Edith Wilson, who was a descendant of Pocahontas. When President Wilson suffered a stroke and had to stay in bed, Mrs. Wilson was the only one who took messages to and from the president. This made some people angry. They thought the first lady was making decisions and running the country herself.

TIMELINE

1913	1914	1917	1918	1920
Henry Ford begins mass production of automobiles	World War I begins in Europe	United States enters World War I	World War I ends	Nineteenth Amendment gives women the right to vote
Hollywood becomes the center of the movie industry				
The kind of zipper we use today is invented				

WARREN G. HARDING [1921–1923]

How hard did Warren G. Harding work as president?

Not very. Harding never wanted to be president, and most people agreed he wasn't a very good one. The poker-playing president once gambled away a whole set of White House china and often played golf instead of working.

I'll see your tea set and raise you a gravy boat.

Harding's feet were probably bigger than any other president's—he wore a size fourteen! George Washington wasn't far behind, having worn a size thirteen.

Was President Harding poisoned?

It's a history mystery. Some people think so because Harding died suddenly in the middle of his term. Word soon got out that the president's men had illegally rented oil fields in Teapot Dome, Wyoming, and kept the money for themselves. Some people suspected that his death was related to this corruption, later known as the Teapot Dome Scandal, but the medical evidence shows that Harding had suffered a heart attack.

☼ TIMELINE

1921
First Miss America contest held in Atlantic City, New Jersey

CALVIN COOLIDGE [1923–1929]

> "AFTER ALL, THE CHIEF BUSINESS OF AMERICA IS BUSINESS."

How did Calvin Coolidge become president in the middle of the night?

Vice President Coolidge was visiting his family in Vermont when President Harding died unexpectedly. Coolidge must have thought he was dreaming when he was awakened and told he was president! His father, a notary public, swore him in at two A.M. in the family farmhouse.

What was President Coolidge's nickname?

Coolidge spoke so little that he earned the nickname "Silent Cal." A woman sitting next to him at a White House dinner told the president she had made a bet she could get him to say more than two words. Cal turned to her and said, "You lose."

Why do we light fireworks on President Coolidge's birthday?

Because he was born on the Fourth of July!

★★★★★★★★★★★★★★

Coolidge and his wife had an unusual collection of pets: a goose, a wallaby, a donkey, a lion cub, a raccoon, two cats, twelve dogs, and lots of birds, including a thrush.

TIMELINE

1923	1925	1927	1928
President Coolidge broadcasts first presidential radio address	First national spelling bee held	Charles Lindbergh makes first solo airplane flight across the Atlantic Ocean	Walt Disney creates first Mickey Mouse cartoon, "Steamboat Willie"
Bulldozer invented		First successful demonstration of how television works, in New York City	

HERBERT HOOVER [1929–1933]

> "... WE SHALL SOON WITH THE HELP OF GOD BE IN SIGHT OF THE DAY WHEN POVERTY WILL BE BANISHED FROM THIS NATION."

What did Herbert Hoover have in common with pirates?

He made his fortune in gold. He didn't steal it, though—he earned it! Hoover was an orphan who became a millionaire in the gold-mining business. Voters liked that he was a self-made man. They also admired the way Hoover had saved millions of lives by getting food to starving Europeans during World War I.

Why did President Hoover have so many towns named after him?

Because he was president at the start of the *Great Depression*, a time when businesses closed and one in four workers lost their jobs. Many had to wait in "bread lines" for food and leave their homes to live in "Hoovervilles," or villages of cardboard shacks. Americans blamed Hoover for the Great Depression even though it wasn't his fault. The president tried to make things better, but he didn't think government should get too involved.

When President Hoover and his wife, Lou, didn't want to be overheard, they spoke to each other in Chinese!

Hoover's son Allan had two pet alligators that sometimes wandered loose around the White House. Do you remember which other president had a pet alligator?

John Quincy Adams

TIMELINE

1929	1930	1930s	1931	1932
Stock market crashes Great Depression begins	Planet Pluto discovered	Severe drought creates Dust Bowl conditions in Great Plains states	"The Star-Spangled Banner" becomes the national anthem	Amelia Earhart flies solo across the Atlantic Ocean

FRANKLIN DELANO ROOSEVELT [1933–1945]

"THE ONLY THING WE HAVE TO FEAR IS FEAR ITSELF."

What kind of deal did President Roosevelt promise America?

A new one. Franklin Delano Roosevelt (who was often referred to by his initials, FDR) promised what he called a New Deal to help Americans suffering during the Great Depression. The New Deal included giving millions of Americans jobs building bridges, dams, schools, and roads; improving parks and housing; and painting murals in public places.

★★★★★★★★★★★★★

When the United States entered World War II in 1941, millions of Americans were needed in the armed forces. President Roosevelt set up programs to recruit and train men—and, for the first time, women—to serve their country. The government also encouraged women to do their part by taking men's jobs on assembly lines. They did, even though many had never worked outside the home.

Could President Roosevelt help you get rid of a sore throat?

No, but Roosevelt did call himself "Dr. New Deal" and later "Dr. Win-the-War." Roosevelt worked with America's allies to keep German leader Adolf Hitler from taking over Europe during World War II. And as he'd done during the Great Depression, FDR boosted spirits with his famous "fireside chats," or casual, comforting speeches over the radio.

It's all relative . . . FDR was related, by blood or marriage, to eleven other presidents: George Washington, John and John Quincy Adams, James Madison, Martin Van Buren, William and Benjamin Harrison, Zachary Taylor, Ulysses S. Grant, Theodore Roosevelt, and William Howard Taft.

FDR was a very superstitious man. He wouldn't sit at a table of thirteen people, and he refused to leave for a trip on a Friday, even though he traveled quite a bit.

What did President Roosevelt ride inside the White House?

a) a skateboard   c) a wheelchair

b) a jet airplane   d) a roller coaster

The answer is letter *c*. FDR had to use a wheelchair or braces because his legs were paralyzed by a disease called polio when he was thirty-nine. FDR joked about his disability, sometimes saying, "Well, got to run!"

What did Roosevelt do that no president had ever done—or will ever do?

He was elected president four times. Even though FDR had been a great president, a few years after he died, a Constitutional amendment was passed that said presidents could serve only two full terms.

★★★★★★★★★★★★★★★★★★★★★★★★

FDR's Scottish terrier, Fala, had something in common with President Zachary Taylor's horse, Whitey. Fala, who went almost everywhere the president did, became so popular that when FDR took the dog on an official trip aboard the USS Baltimore, sailors cut hairs off the dog as souvenirs. They cut so many that little Fala was left almost completely bald!

What if you wrote a letter to First Lady Eleanor Roosevelt?

There was a good chance she'd write you back—even though she got about two hundred fifty thousand letters a year. The well-loved Mrs. Roosevelt also worked tirelessly to help the unemployed and disadvantaged, especially women, African Americans, and young people. She toured the country giving speeches, visiting the poorest neighborhoods, and even inspecting the depths of coal mines to see if they were safe!

What will we call the husband of the first female president? The first gentleman?

★★★★★★★★★★★★★★★★

FDR's favorite hobby was collecting stamps. He started collecting when he was eleven and by the end of his life had more than twenty-five thousand. That licks most collections!

TIMELINE

1933	1934	1937	1938
FDR appoints first female cabinet officer, Secretary of Labor Frances Perkins	Nylon invented	Golden Gate Bridge dedicated	Xerox machine invented

1939	1941
FDR becomes first president to appear on TV World War II begins in Europe Helicopter invented	U.S. enters World War II when the Japanese bomb Pearl Harbor in Hawaii Mt. Rushmore completed Paperback books introduced

HARRY S TRUMAN [1945–1953]

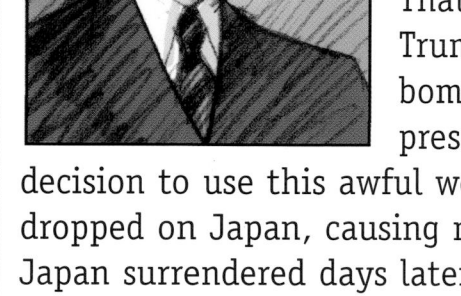

"THE BUCK STOPS HERE."

What was "the most terrible bomb in the history of the world"?

That's what President Harry S Truman said about the atomic bomb. Soon after Truman became president, he made the difficult decision to use this awful weapon. Two atomic bombs were dropped on Japan, causing mass destruction and death. Japan surrendered days later, ending World War II.

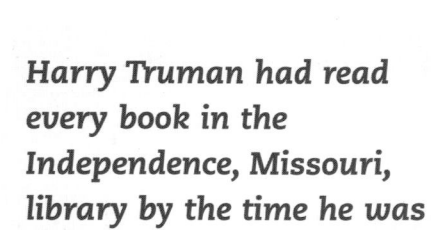

The sign on Truman's desk, THE BUCK STOPS HERE, meant that the president couldn't pass his responsibilities off onto anyone else.

Was the Cold War fought at the North Pole?

No. And it wasn't a war against getting sick, either. The "Cold War" wasn't really a war but a competition between two kinds of government: *democracy*, or government by the people, and *communism*, or government that owns everything and is very controlling. Truman promised to help any country that was fighting communism. When communist North Korea invaded South Korea in 1950, President Truman sent troops to help the South Koreans.

Harry Truman had read every book in the Independence, Missouri, library by the time he was fifteen. He read a lot because his thick glasses made it hard for him to play sports.

The Buck Stops Here.

TIMELINE

1945	1947	1949	1950	1951	1952
World War II ends	Jackie Robinson is the first African American to play major-league baseball	Bikinis invented	American troops fight in the Korean War Charles Schulz creates *Peanuts* comic strip	Some television stations begin broadcasting in color	3-D movies invented

DWIGHT D. EISENHOWER [1953–1961]

"NO EASY PROBLEMS EVER COME TO THE PRESIDENT OF THE UNITED STATES."

Who liked Ike?

Nearly everyone. Ike was Dwight D. Eisenhower, the general responsible for the victory won by the United States and its allies in World War II. Ike was a hero, and lots of people wanted him to run for president. When he did, they cheered, "We like Ike!"

Were the Little Rock Nine a rock-and-roll band?

No, they were a group of nine students in Little Rock, Arkansas, who, in 1957, were the first African Americans to attend an all-white public school. Before that, African Americans and whites had often gone to *segregated*, or separate, schools. Eisenhower sent troops to protect the African American students.

What did Eisenhower do that was out of this world?

He signed a bill that created NASA, the National Aeronautics and Space Administration. After Russia surprised the world by launching *Sputnik*, the first man-made object to circle the Earth, the United States began a "space race" with Russia to discover new things about outer space.

TIMELINE

1953	1954	1955	1959
President Eisenhower helps end Korean War	U.S. Supreme Court, in *Brown v. Board of Education*, says segregated schools are unconstitutional	Montgomery, Alabama, bus boycott protests segregation Disneyland, the world's first theme park, opens in California	Alaska and Hawaii become forty-ninth and fiftieth states

JOHN F. KENNEDY [1961–1963]

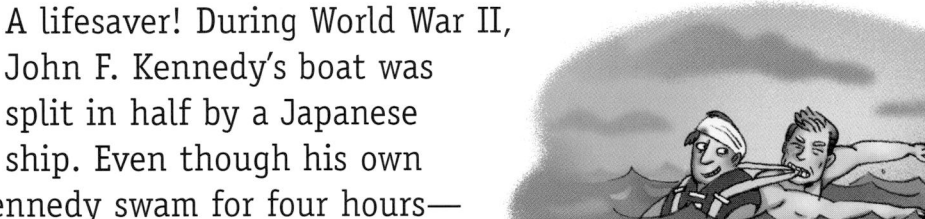

> "ASK NOT WHAT YOUR COUNTRY CAN DO FOR YOU, ASK WHAT YOU CAN DO FOR YOUR COUNTRY."

President Kennedy was like what kind of candy?

A lifesaver! During World War II, John F. Kennedy's boat was split in half by a Japanese ship. Even though his own back was badly hurt, Kennedy swam for four hours—with the strap of one of his crew members' life jackets in his teeth—to bring the man to safety.

Why did women all over the world copy First Lady Jackie Kennedy?

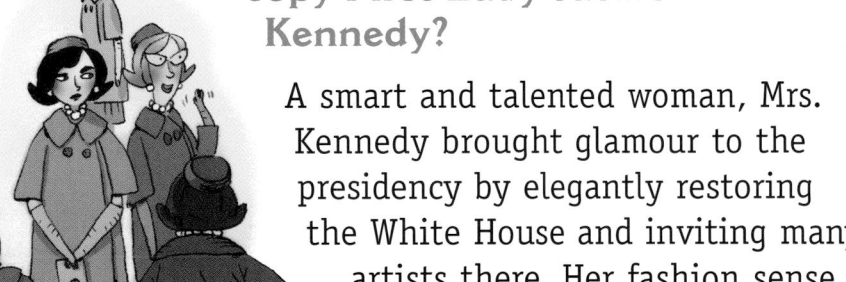

A smart and talented woman, Mrs. Kennedy brought glamour to the presidency by elegantly restoring the White House and inviting many artists there. Her fashion sense was copied around the world.

Kennedy was the:
— *first president to have been a Boy Scout*
— *first Catholic president*
— *youngest president to be elected to office*

What shocked America in the middle of Kennedy's term?

Kennedy was assassinated during a motorcade in Dallas, Texas, by a man named Lee Harvey Oswald. Americans were stunned by the loss of the young and popular president.

TIMELINE

1961	1962	1963
Alan Shepard is first U.S. astronaut in space	Kennedy avoids nuclear war by settling Cuban missile crisis with Soviet Union	Martin Luther King, Jr., leads two hundred thousand African Americans and whites in the March on Washington to promote civil rights and delivers his "I Have a Dream" speech First Polaroid color pictures

LYNDON B. JOHNSON [1963–1969]

"WE HAVE TALKED LONG ENOUGH IN THIS COUNTRY ABOUT EQUAL RIGHTS."

Was President Johnson an auto mechanic, a grape picker, or a high school teacher?

Before he became president, Lyndon B. Johnson was all those things! He grew up in a poor family, and shined shoes and trapped animals as a child to earn extra money.

What was President Johnson's dream?

Johnson wanted America to be a Great Society, where everyone was equal. He protected the voting rights of African Americans and tried to keep them from being mistreated because of the color of their skin. To aid the poor, he declared a War on Poverty and created Medicare and Medicaid to help people pay their medical bills.

Why did college students burn American flags during Johnson's presidency?

Because they were angry that Americans were fighting and dying in the Vietnam War. President Johnson had sent troops to help the South Vietnamese fight the communist North Vietnamese. Many Americans thought South Vietnam should fight its own war.

TIMELINE

1964	1965	1967	1968
United States enters Vietnam War	Civil rights leader Malcolm X assassinated in New York City	Johnson is first president to appoint an African American, Thurgood Marshall, to the Supreme Court First Super Bowl played	Martin Luther King, Jr., assassinated in Memphis, Tennessee

RICHARD M. NIXON [1969–1974]

"AT EVERY TURN WE HAVE BEEN BESET BY THOSE WHO FIND EVERYTHING WRONG WITH AMERICA AND LITTLE THAT IS RIGHT."

How many states did Richard M. Nixon visit?

All fifty. President Nixon was the first president to do that. He was also the first to visit communist China.

Why did President Nixon give up his job?

Nixon was the first and only person to *resign*, or give up, his job as U.S. president. He resigned because he was caught in a scandal called Watergate. During his reelection campaign, five of his supporters tried to steal information from his opponent's offices at the Watergate Hotel. Nixon said he wasn't involved, but tape recordings proved he was lying.

★★★★★★★★★★★★★

Nixon was called "Tricky Dick" for his aggressive way of winning his Senate seat in 1950.

Would Nixon have made a good football coach?

Probably not! President Nixon called the coach of the Miami Dolphins before Super Bowl VI to recommend a play. Unfortunately, the play didn't work.

TIMELINE

1969	1970	1971	1973
Neil Armstrong first to walk on the moon	First Earth Day celebrated Pong, the first video game, invented	Twenty-sixth Amendment lowers voting age to eighteen	Vice President Spiro Agnew resigns U.S. troops leave Vietnam but war continues

GERALD R. FORD [1974–1977]

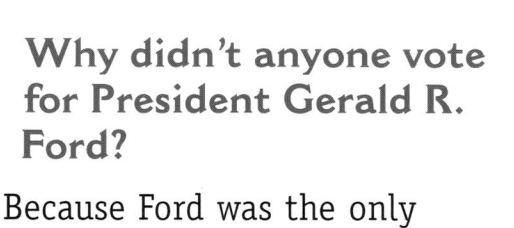

> "MY FELLOW AMERICANS, OUR LONG NATIONAL NIGHTMARE IS OVER."

Why didn't anyone vote for President Gerald R. Ford?

Because Ford was the only president who didn't run for either president or vice president. Nixon chose Ford to replace Vice President Spiro Agnew when Agnew left office in 1973. Ford then became president when Nixon resigned.

Thanks for your vote, citizen.

Uh, I didn't vote for you.

That's OK, nobody did.

Why did President Ford let Nixon off the hook?

Ford thought it was best for Americans to put Nixon's scandal behind them. So he *pardoned*, or publicly forgave, his former boss. This made many people angry, because they thought Nixon should have to face up to his crimes.

What made Ford a model president?

While he was in law school, Ford was a fashion model who appeared on the cover of *Cosmopolitan* and in the pages of *Look* magazine. He also helped create a modeling agency. Before that, Ford was an all-star football player at the University of Michigan who received offers to play professional football from the Detroit Lions and the Green Bay Packers.

President Ford's daughter Susan held her high school prom at the White House.

Future Prez MAGAZINE

10¢

Four Score & Twenty New Hair Styles

10 Hot Looks for the Commander in Chief

TIMELINE

1975	1976
Vietnam War ends	*Viking* spacecraft lands on Mars
	United States celebrates its two hundredth birthday

JIMMY CARTER [1977–1981]

> "IF I EVER TELL A LIE, I WANT YOU TO COME AND TAKE ME OUT OF THE WHITE HOUSE."

Why were the Carters so nuts about their family business?

Because the family business *was* nuts—peanuts! Jimmy Carter grew up on a peanut farm in Georgia and sold peanuts on the street as a boy. Even though the Carters were better off than most of their neighbors, they didn't have electricity or running water.

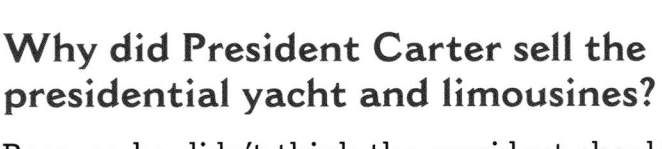

Why did President Carter sell the presidential yacht and limousines?

Because he didn't think the president should be treated differently from any other American. Carter made sure everyone called him Jimmy, not James Earl Carter, Jr. He sometimes carried his own luggage, and he told his bodyguards to stop opening doors for him. Carter believed in human rights and worked for peace around the world.

Carter was a speed reader who could read and understand nearly two thousand words per minute!

Carter was the first president born in a hospital. All those before him had been born at home.

TRUE OR FALSE President Carter's family helped him run the country.

True. The Carters had "family councils" in which First Lady Rosalyn and the four Carter children gave the president their thoughts on all kinds of issues—including how to improve the school lunch program!

TIMELINE

1977	1978	1980
First successful personal computer, Apple II, introduced	First "test-tube baby" born Carter facilitates Camp David Peace Accord between Egypt and Israel	Mount St. Helens volcano erupts in Washington State

RONALD REAGAN [1981–1989]

> "IT IS TIME FOR US TO REALIZE THAT WE ARE TOO GREAT A NATION TO LIMIT OURSELVES TO SMALL DREAMS."

TRUE OR FALSE **Ronald Reagan was a movie star before he became president.**

True! Ronald Reagan was a radio sportscaster, a TV host, and a Hollywood star who acted in more than fifty movies. Before that, he'd been a lifeguard and claimed to have rescued seventy-seven people.

What birthday did President Reagan celebrate sixteen days after he was inaugurated?

His seventieth. That made Reagan the oldest president to be elected. His old-fashioned, cheerful ways made people feel good about America, even if things weren't always perfect.

Was Reagan's favorite food really . . . beans?

Yep. But not string beans or lima beans—jelly beans. Reagan kept a jar of them on his desk and picked out the coconut ones for himself. As governor of California, he used to take a jar to meetings, and he said his advisors could hardly make a decision without passing it around!

When did presidents start wearing bulletproof vests?

After a madman tried to kill President Reagan outside a Washington hotel in 1981. Reagan was shot in the chest but survived. Although the shooting was serious, Reagan made people smile when he joked, "I just forgot to duck!" Since then, presidents often wear bulletproof vests in public. America's president is one of the world's most heavily guarded men.

Who is Ronald Reagan II?

He is really one of Reagan's sons. But he was also a fish! While President Reagan was recovering from the shooting, a ten-year-old boy sent him a goldfish named Ronald Reagan II. Ronald II lived for more than three years.

Nancy Reagan tasted all the food that was served to White House guests while her husband was president.

First Lady Nancy Reagan told children to "Just Say No" to:

a) roller-coaster rides   c) scary movies

b) pie-eating contests   d) drugs

Drugs. Mrs. Reagan spoke to young people all over the country about the dangers of using and becoming addicted to drugs.

TIMELINE

1981	1983	1984	1985	1986
American hostages released after more than a year as prisoners in Iran	Sally Ride is first female U.S. astronaut in space	Geraldine Ferraro is first female vice presidential candidate from a major party	Halley's Comet passes by Earth	Space shuttle *Challenger* explodes
President Reagan appoints first female Supreme Court justice, Sandra Day O'Connor				

GEORGE BUSH [1989–1993]

"READ MY LIPS: NO NEW TAXES."

How many lives does George Bush have?

Some might say he has five. As a World War II fighter pilot, Bush somehow survived four plane crashes. He received the Distinguished Flying Cross for his bravery. For a while, the nineteen-year-old was the youngest pilot in the U.S. Navy.

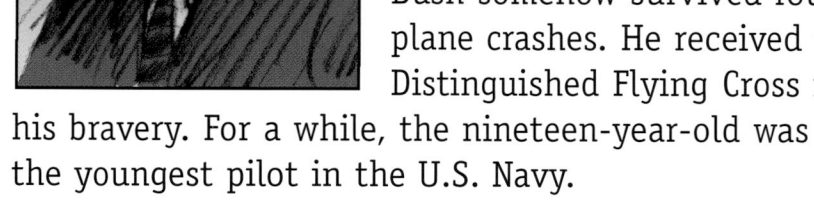

Whoops. Again.

Could weathermen predict Desert Storm?

No, because the "storm" didn't have anything to do with weather. Desert Storm was the code name for a war in the Persian Gulf area. The war was fought to force Iraq to leave its neighbor Kuwait, which it had invaded. If Iraq had won, its leader, Saddam Hussein, would have controlled a large amount of oil. Desert Storm was a short war and a big victory for the United States and its allies.

SCRAM! And take your little carrot friends with you, too!

What did President Bush ban from the White House?

Hint: It looks like tiny green trees. It's broccoli! President Bush said, "I'm the president of the United States, and I'm not going to eat any more broccoli!" That made broccoli growers so mad, they sent him truckloads of the vegetable.

TIMELINE

1991	1991
Cold War ends with the breakup of the Soviet Union	Persian Gulf War

WILLIAM JEFFERSON CLINTON [1993–2001]

> "THERE IS NOTHING WRONG WITH AMERICA THAT CANNOT BE CURED BY WHAT IS RIGHT WITH AMERICA."

When did Bill Clinton start "practicing" to be president?

Clinton always knew he wanted to be president one day. He ran for so many offices in his high school student government that his principal said he couldn't run for any more! As a teenager, William Jefferson Clinton shook hands with President Kennedy at the White House.

Why did some people say America got two leaders for the price of one?

Because President Clinton's wife, Hillary, had so much political responsibility. Mrs. Clinton was a successful lawyer before her husband asked her to lead his task force on health care. The first lady was especially interested in family and children's issues. Some people said she could have been president herself.

Clinton played his saxophone on national TV during the 1992 presidential campaign.

What did President Clinton say was one of America's bad habits?

Expecting "something for nothing." Clinton got Congress to pass welfare reform, which said that people on *welfare*, or government support for poor people, had to try to find a job.

What did President Clinton have in common with President Andrew Johnson?

Clinton was the second president to be impeached, for lying about his relationship with a White House intern. Clinton wasn't convicted either and didn't have to leave office.

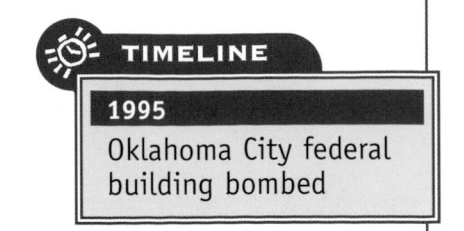

☀ TIMELINE

1995
Oklahoma City federal building bombed

GEORGE W. BUSH [2001-]

"THE MOST IMPORTANT TASKS OF A DEMOCRACY ARE DONE BY EVERYONE."

Why was George W. Bush nicknamed "Quincy" after he won the presidential election?

★ ★ ★ ★ ★ ★ ★ ★ ★ ★ ★ ★ ★ ★

Because President Bush has something in common with John Quincy Adams, America's sixth president. (For a hint of what that might be, turn to page 17, then to page 60.) George W. Bush is the second American president to be the son of a former president. When he was elected, his father, the first President Bush, started calling him "Quincy" as a joke. To avoid confusion with his father, many people also call him "W."

If you want to follow in your parent's presidential footsteps, it seems to help if you share his name!

(For a hint of what that might be, turn to page 17, then to page 60.)

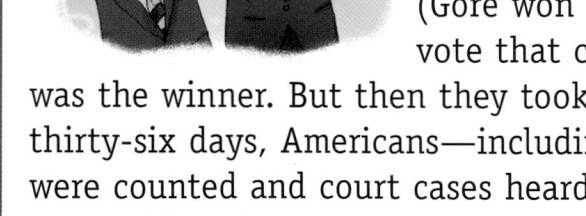

We win, again!

Why was George W. Bush declared president twice—in the same election?

Because the race between Bush and his opponent, Al Gore, was so close that it was difficult to tell who won the electoral vote. (Gore won the popular vote by half a million, but it's the electoral vote that counts.) On election night, television stations said Bush was the winner. But then they took it back, saying the race was "too close to call." For thirty-six days, Americans—including the candidates—waited in suspense while votes were counted and court cases heard. In the end, Bush was declared the winner again. This was the fourth time in U.S. history, and the first time in more than 100 years, that the president hadn't won the popular vote.

What did George W. Bush want to be when he grew up?

Not the president, but a major-league baseball player. Though his dream never came true, Bush did own part of the Texas Rangers professional baseball team until 1998. As spokesman for the team, he had baseball cards made of himself!

Can't I borrow just one?

The president has a collection of 250 signed baseballs!

Presidents and Their Vice Presidents

President Vice President	Years	President Vice President	Years
George Washington	1789–1797	Millard Fillmore	1850–1853
John Adams	1789–1797	Franklin Pierce	1853–1857
John Adams	1797–1801	William R. King	1853
Thomas Jefferson	1797–1801	James Buchanan	1857–1861
Thomas Jefferson	1801–1809	John C. Breckinridge	1857–1861
Aaron Burr	1801–1805	Abraham Lincoln	1861–1865
George Clinton	1805–1809	Hannibal Hamlin	1861–1865
James Madison	1809–1817	Andrew Johnson	1865
George Clinton	1809–1812	Andrew Johnson	1865–1869
Elbridge Gerry	1813–1814	Ulysses S. Grant	1869–1877
James Monroe	1817–1825	Schuyler Colfax	1869–1873
Daniel D. Tompkins	1817–1825	Henry Wilson	1873–1875
John Quincy Adams	1825–1829	Rutherford B. Hayes	1877–1881
John C. Calhoun	1825–1829	William A. Wheeler	1877–1881
Andrew Jackson	1829–1837	James A. Garfield	1881
John C. Calhoun	1829–1832	Chester A. Arthur	1881
Martin Van Buren	1833–1837	Chester A. Arthur	1881–1885
Martin Van Buren	1837–1841	Grover Cleveland	1885–1889
Richard M. Johnson	1837–1841	Thomas A. Hendricks	1885
William Henry Harrison	1841	Benjamin Harrison	1889–1893
John Tyler	1841	Levi P. Morton	1889–1893
John Tyler	1841–1845	Grover Cleveland	1893–1897
James K. Polk	1845–1849	Adlai E. Stevenson	1893–1897
George M. Dallas	1845–1849	William McKinley	1897–1901
Zachary Taylor	1849–1850	Garret A. Hobart	1897–1899
Millard Fillmore	1849–1850	Theodore Roosevelt	1901

President Vice President	Years	President Vice President	Years
Theodore Roosevelt	1901–1909	John F. Kennedy	1961–1963
Charles W. Fairbanks	1905–1909	Lyndon B. Johnson	1961–1963
William H. Taft	1909–1913	Lyndon B. Johnson	1963–1969
James S. Sherman	1909–1912	Hubert H. Humphrey	1965–1969
Woodrow Wilson	1913–1921	Richard M. Nixon	1969–1974
Thomas R. Marshall	1913–1921	Spiro Agnew	1969–1973
Warren G. Harding	1921–1923	Gerald R. Ford	1973–1974
Calvin Coolidge	1921–1923	Gerald R. Ford	1974–1977
Calvin Coolidge	1923–1929	Nelson A. Rockefeller	1974–1977
Charles G. Dawes	1925–1929	Jimmy Carter	1977–1981
Herbert Hoover	1929–1933	Walter F. Mondale	1977–1981
Charles Curtis	1929–1933	Ronald Reagan	1981–1989
Franklin Delano Roosevelt	1933–1945	George Bush	1981–1989
John N. Garner	1933–1941	George Bush	1989–1993
Henry A. Wallace	1941–1945	J. Danforth Quayle	1989–1993
Harry S Truman	1945	William Jefferson Clinton	1993–2001
Harry S Truman	1945–1953	Albert Gore	1993–2001
Alben W. Barkley	1949–1953	George W. Bush	2001–
Dwight D. Eisenhower	1953–1961	Richard Cheney	2001–
Richard M. Nixon	1953–1961		